SONG TITLE	PAGE NUMBER	TRACK WITH MELODY CUE	TRACK ACCOMPANIMENT ONLY
BE OUR GUEST	2	1	2
THE BELLS OF NOTRE DAME	4	3	4
CAN YOU FEEL THE LOVE TONIGHT	6	5	6
I JUST CAN'T WAIT TO BE KING	8	7	8
COLORS OF THE WIND	10	9	10
FRIEND LIKE ME	12	11	12
PART OF YOUR WORLD	14	13	14
UNDER THE SEA	16	15	16
REFLECTION	18	17	18
YOU'LL BE IN MY HEART	19	19	20
YOU'VE GOT A FRIEND IN ME	20	21	22
ZERO TO HERO	22	23	24
B♭ Tuning Notes		25	

ISBN 0-634-00067-5

Wonderland Music Company, Inc.
Walt Disney Music Company

DISTRIBUTED BY

7777 W. BLUEMOUND RD. P.O. BOX 13819 MILWAUKEE, WI 53213

Disney characters and artwork © Disney Enterprises, Inc.

For all works contained herein:
Unauthorized copying, arranging, adapting, recording or public performance is an infringement of copyright.
Infringers are liable under the law.

Visit Hal Leonard Online at
www.halleonard.com

BE OUR GUEST

from Walt Disney's BEAUTY AND THE BEAST

Lyrics by HOWARD ASHMAN
Music by ALAN MENKEN

CD
1: With melody cue
2: Accompaniment only

FLUTE

© 1991 Walt Disney Music Company and Wonderland Music Company, Inc.
All Rights Reserved   Used by Permission

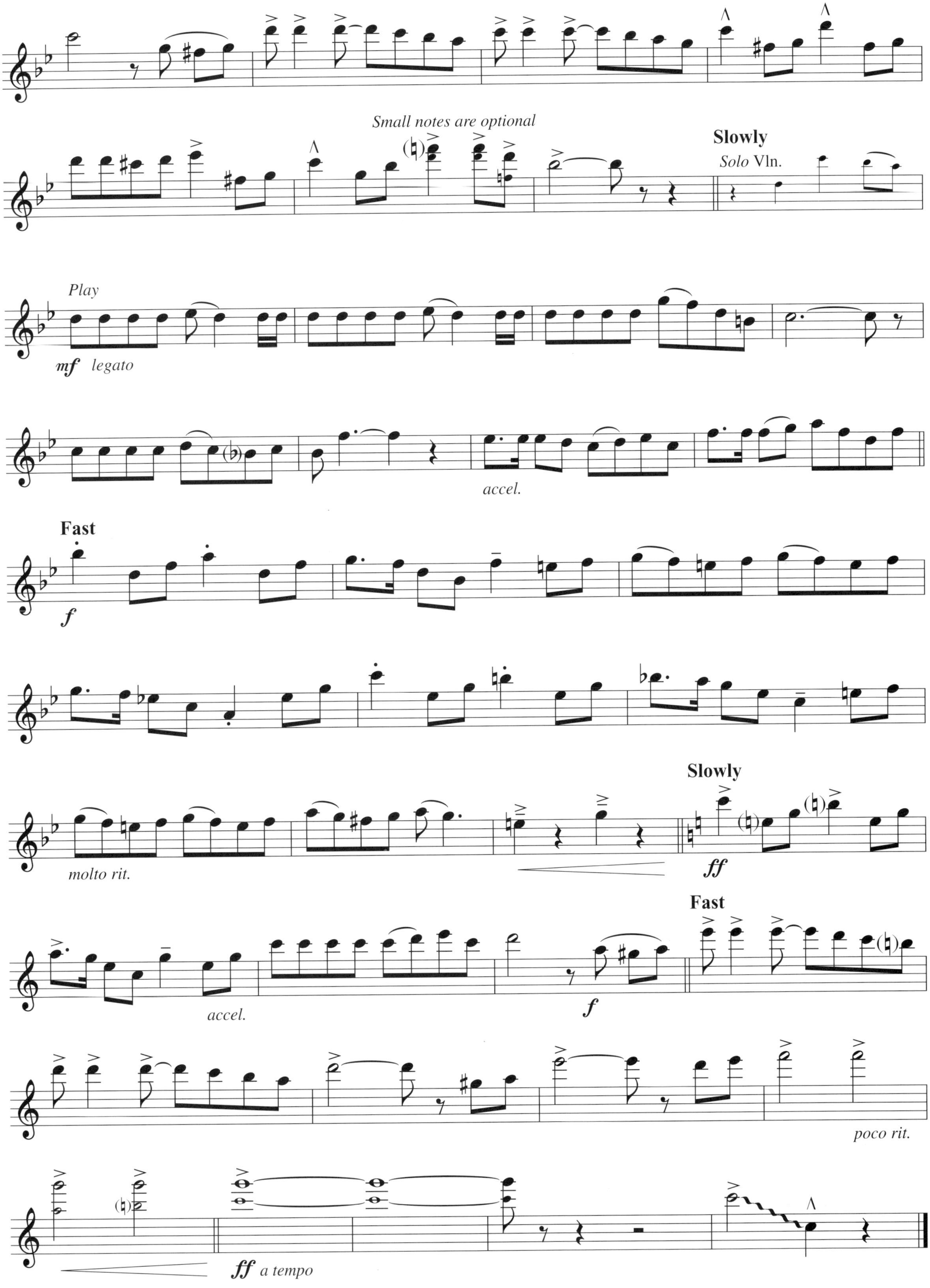
Small notes are optional
Slowly
Solo Vln.
Play
mf legato
accel.
Fast
f
molto rit.
Slowly
ff
Fast
accel.
f
poco rit.
ff a tempo

THE BELLS OF NOTRE DAME

from Walt Disney's THE HUNCHBACK OF NOTRE DAME

Music by ALAN MENKEN
Lyrics by STEPHEN SCHWARTZ

CD
3: With melody cue
4: Accompaniment only

FLUTE

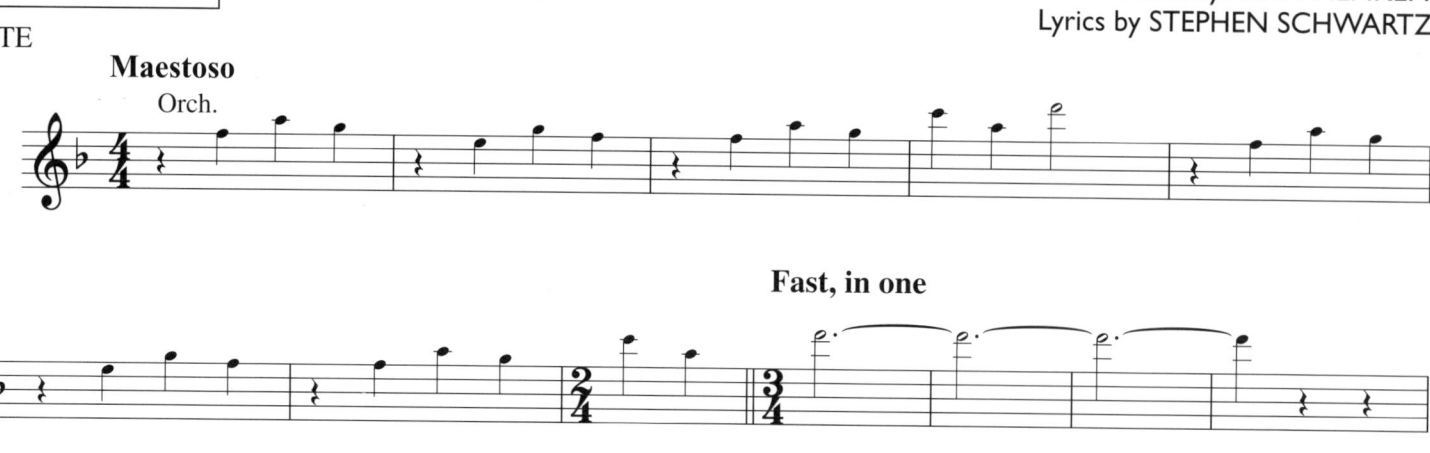

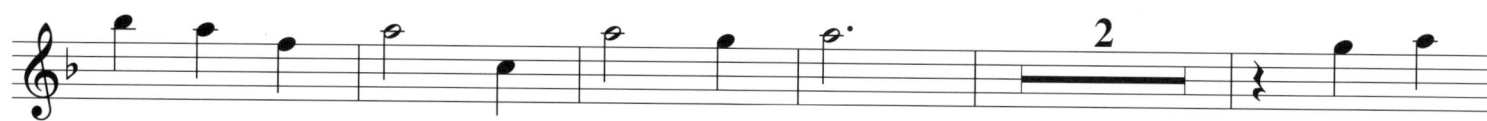

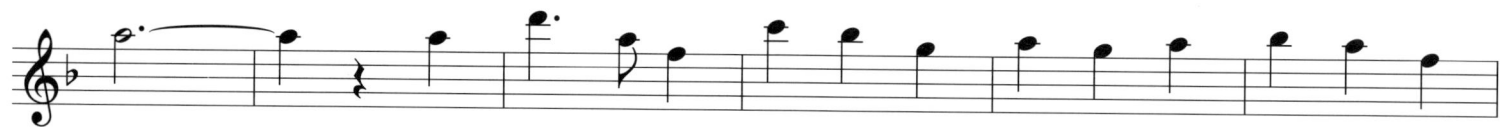
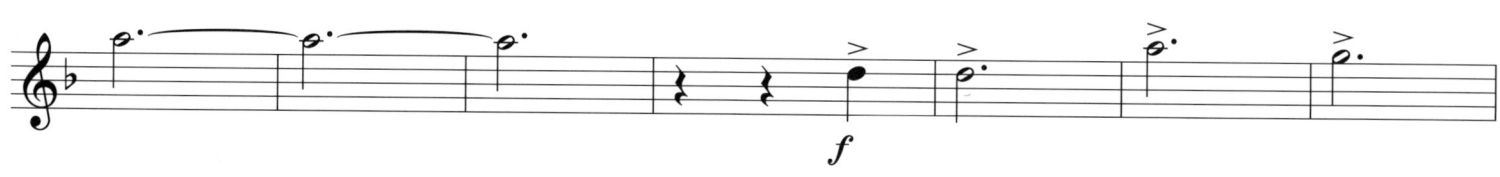

© 1996 WonderLand Music Company, Inc. and Walt Disney Music Company
All Rights Reserved   Used by Permission

CAN YOU FEEL THE LOVE TONIGHT

from Walt Disney Pictures' THE LION KING

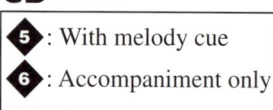

Music by ELTON JOHN
Lyrics by TIM RICE

FLUTE

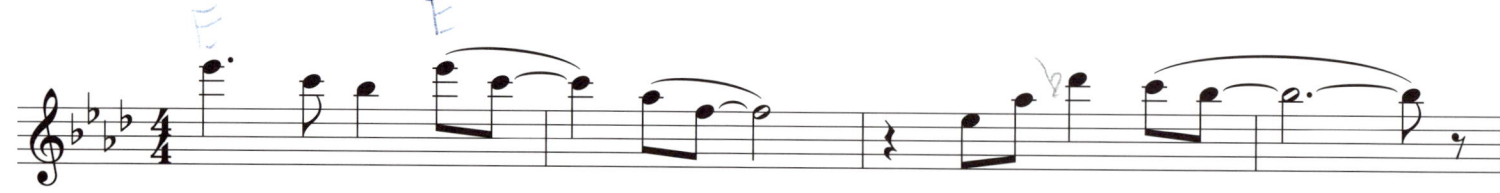

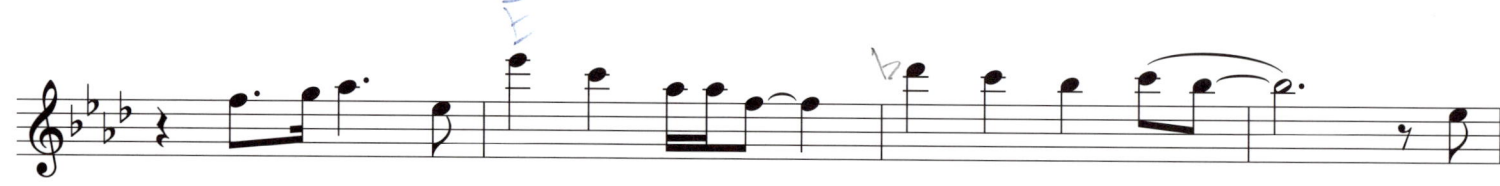

© 1994 WonderIand Music Company, Inc.
All Rights Reserved   Used by Permission

I JUST CAN'T WAIT TO BE KING

from Walt Disney Pictures' THE LION KING

CD
- 7: With melody cue
- 8: Accompaniment only

Music by ELTON JOHN
Lyrics by TIM RICE

FLUTE

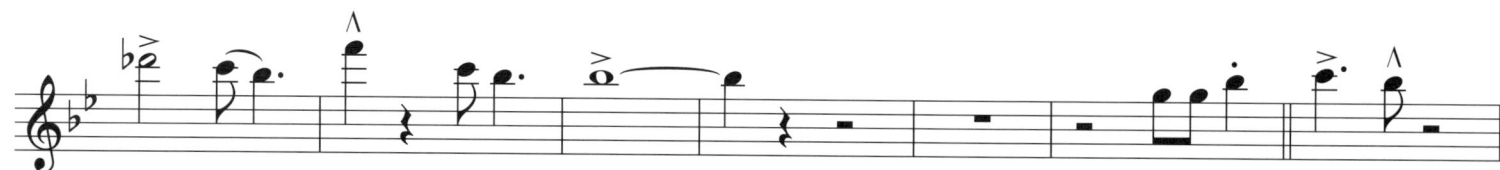

© 1994 Wonderland Music Company, Inc.
All Rights Reserved   Used by Permission

COLORS OF THE WIND
from Walt Disney's POCAHONTAS

Music by ALAN MENKEN
Lyrics by STEPHEN SCHWARTZ

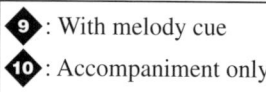

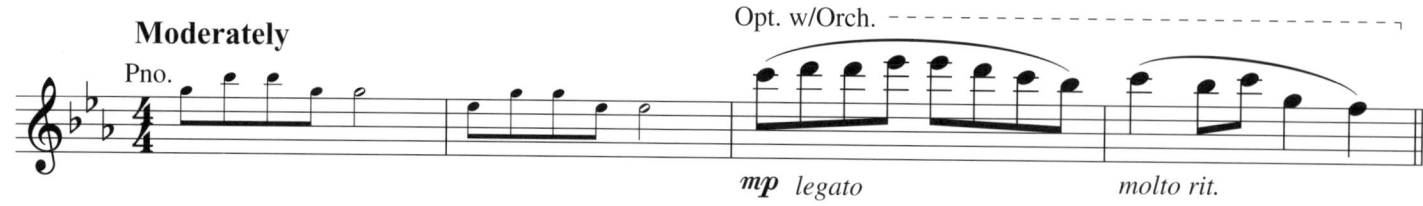

© 1995 Wonderland Music Company, Inc. and Walt Disney Music Company
All Rights Reserved   Used by Permission

PART OF YOUR WORLD
from Walt Disney's THE LITTLE MERMAID

Lyrics by HOWARD ASHMAN
Music by ALAN MENKEN

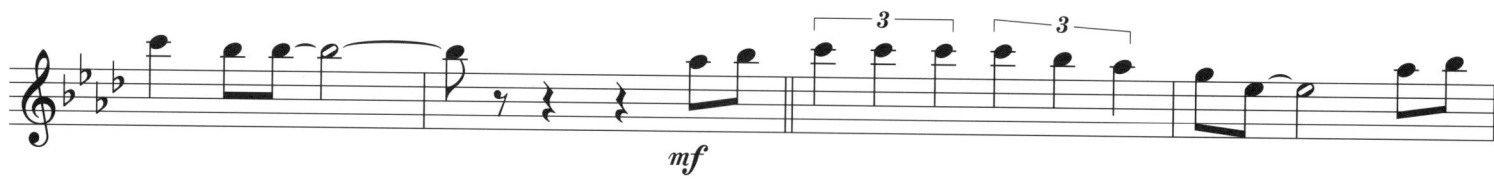
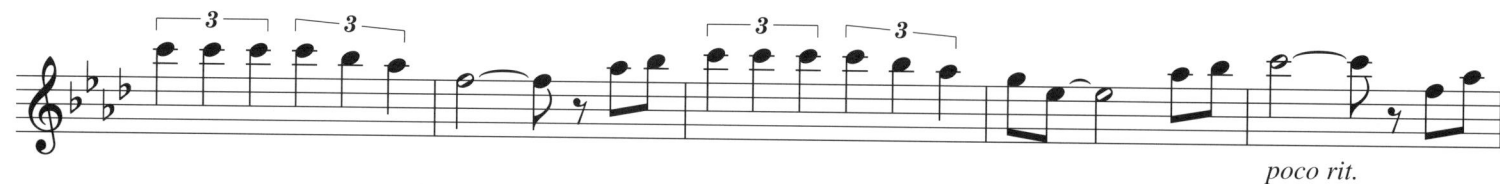
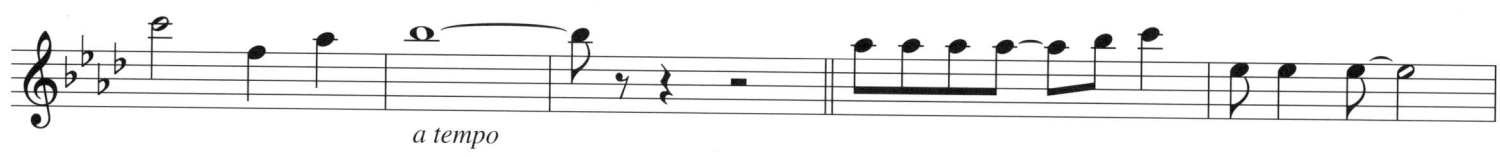

© 1988 Walt Disney Music Company and Wonderland Music Company, Inc.
All Rights Reserved   Used by Permission

YOU'LL BE IN MY HEART

(Pop Version)

from Walt Disney Pictures' TARZAN™

CD

19 : With melody cue

20 : Accompaniment only

Words and Music by
PHIL COLLINS

FLUTE

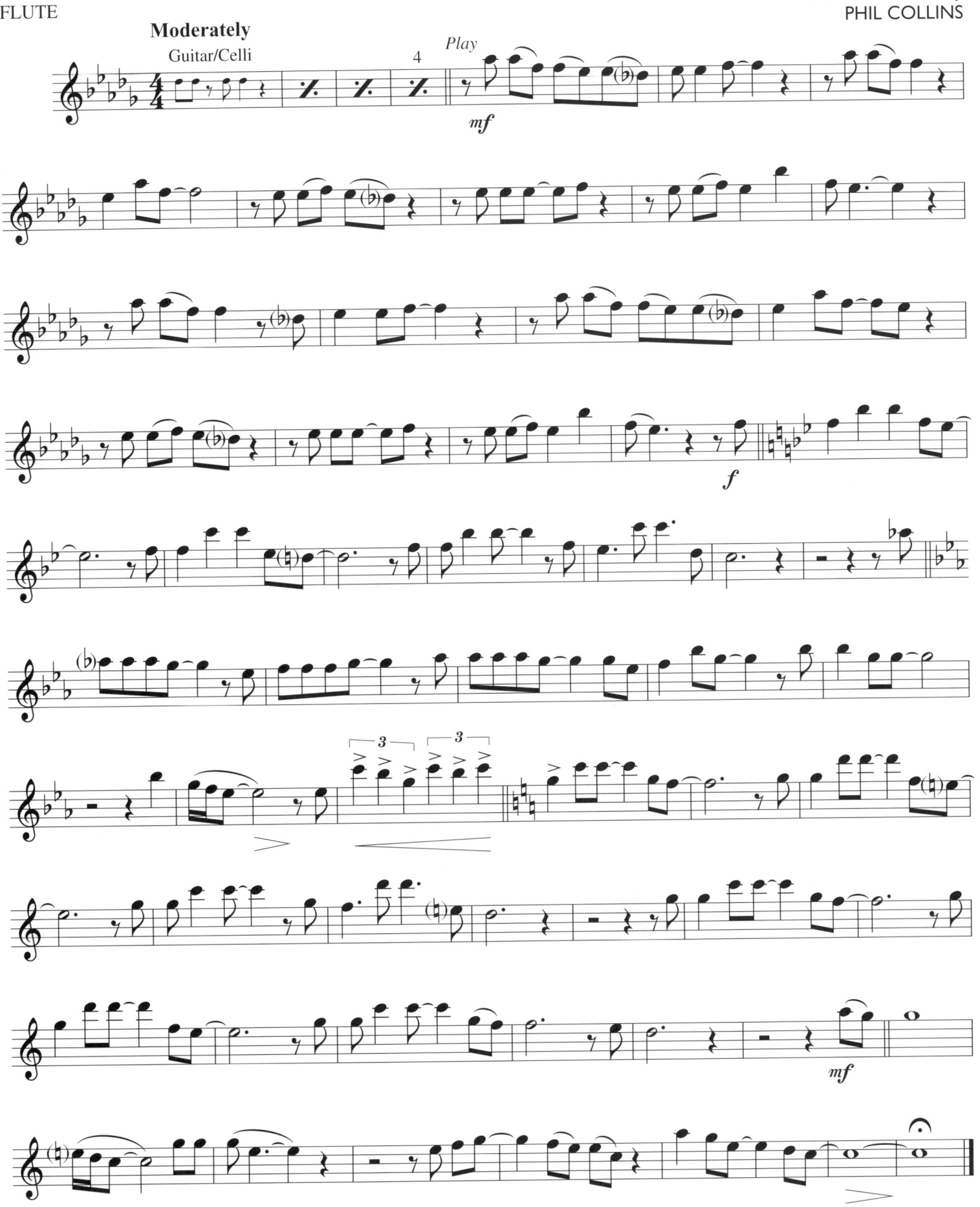

YOU'VE GOT A FRIEND IN ME

from Walt Disney's TOY STORY

CD

21: With melody cue
22: Accompaniment only

Music and Lyrics by
RANDY NEWMAN

FLUTE

Easy Shuffle

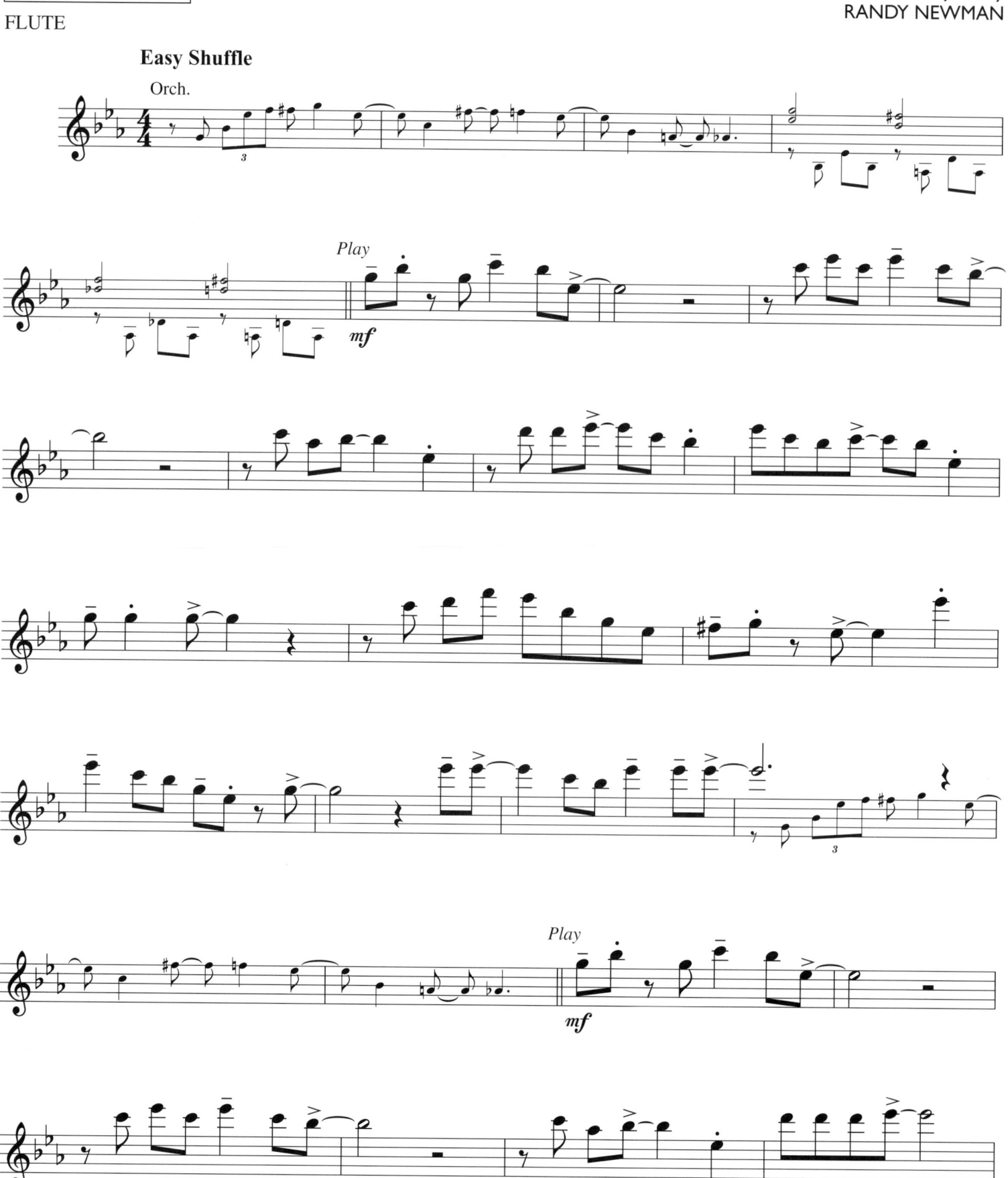

ZERO TO HERO
from Walt Disney Pictures' HERCULES

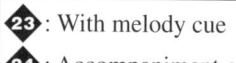

Music by ALAN MENKEN
Lyrics by DAVID ZIPPEL

Much faster "a la Baptist Church"